THE WILDERN[...] [...]HICH

THE WILDERNESS
AFTER WHICH

||||||||||||||||||||||||||||||||||||||||||||||||||||||||||

L. S. KLATT

OTIS BOOKS | SEISMICITY EDITIONS
The Graduate Writing program
Otis College of Art and Design
LOS ANGELES ● 2016

Book design and typesetting: Esther S. Lee

ISBN-13: 978-0-9860836-3-1

OTIS BOOKS | SEISMICITY EDITIONS
The Graduate Writing program
Otis College of Art and Design
9045 Lincoln Boulevard
Los Angeles, CA 90045

http://www.otis.edu/graduate-writing/otis-books
seismicity@otis.edu

For my brother, Larry, banker of the utmost treasure

CONTENTS

THE CORPORATION

15	STARBUCKS
16	DEERE
17	THE TRACTOR
18	THE FARM, 1922
19	CATERPILLAR
20	GENERAL MOTORS
21	THE EUNUCH'S HAPPY VEHICLE
22	KELLOGG'S
23	HONEYWELL
24	THE IMPERATIVES AS THEY OCCUR
25	DOW
26	KRAFT
27	FOX
28	HORNBOOK
29	APPLE
30	REMARKABLE PEARS
31	PLAINTIVE
32	WHAT I MEAN BY CHARLES NORTH
33	THE OHIO ELEMENT
34	THE SAPIENT
35	CALVIN KLEIN
36	DIXON TICONDEROGA
37	RED CAPE, YELLOW MANTLE, VIOLET TAIL, BLUE FEET, GREEN MOUTH
38	THE DOOR TO UKULELE
39	THE BEATS
40	THE BODY SHOP
41	THE SIDEREAL MESSENGER

The Consumer

45	The Wilderness After Which
46	The Angler
47	The Thrower
48	Barker
49	Hallmark
50	Chase
51	Big Sur
52	Plutocrats
53	David Foster Wallace
54	Dole
55	Johnson & Johnson
56	Ford
57	Small Machines Made of Words
58	Big Shot
59	The Insomniac
60	Lost Dialect
61	Original Mule
62	False Cow
63	McDonald's
64	The God Bug
65	True Value
66	The Golden Days of Textiles
67	Time Signature for Sapphire Tuba
68	The Sublime Hiss
69	The Station
70	Amazon
71	Nike

THE CITY

75	THE CITY, 1912
76	GENERAL ELECTRIC
77	PEPSICO
78	THE CENSOR
79	THE MARTYR'S MERRY CHERRY BOMB
80	UNITED
81	LACHRYMOSE
82	GOODWILL
83	GOODYEAR
84	DISCOVER
85	THE SNOW PYRAMID
86	IF RIGHTLY THE VIRGIN IS CALLED
87	THE REVELATION OF ST. ROBOT
88	MARATHON
89	TOMATILLO
90	THE HUNGER
91	DISCLOSURE
92	WHEREABOUTS
93	INCESSANT BIRD REVEALING THE UNKNOWN
94	NIGHT IS HAPLESS RABBIT IS LIPPY
95	BLACK SWANS
96	MYSTIC HORSE
97	THE IRON EWE
98	THE OVERCOAT
99	YAHOO
100	PENGUIN
101	UTMOST LEOPARD

Never had there been such splendor in the great city,
for the victorious war had brought plenty in its train,
and the merchants had flocked thither...
— F. Scott Fitzgerald

They were devout in the chapel of sales;
advertising was their Holy Spirit.
— Ansel Adams

THE CORPORATION

Starbucks

Lonely reader, reading the waves, you are not a cynosure, merely trendy, perhaps a trendsetter. It is not you who craves attention or aggression; your motives are benign, at worst commercial, some would say transactional. And thinking of others, as you do, there is an altruism. Something is brewing, you want to be a part of it, so you train your eyes on conquest, the next gambit. Does your magnitude diminish?–will you perish? These are questions, natural enough. Peradventure, the best is yet. Can you claim it, all the while endure the chase, a chase so wild, & so remorseless the havoc? You count yourself corporate, immortal in community yet disposable in essence. Hence it is that, until your time has elapsed, you confabulate. Not a tame charmer of words but a crusader after perils. For bottom line, dear reader, be practical; the armchair enterprise is soon at sea, yaws. Seesaw anchorage.

DEERE

Where I live, the grass menstruates, & the strawberry bleeds, & tongues of fawns are raked from the prairie, & all this occurs, or has occurred, in my backyard, which I will assign the name Illinois. Illinois is known for its roses & hummingbird feeder, & when hurting I like to sit on its fringe & watch the breezes bend the wrist bones of the sugar maple. The maple touches Illinois with hands, hands that also finesse the plastic flamingo, which is trembling. Where I live (what I live for) can be cut with a John Deere.

The Tractor

The unexpected quail gather behind the tractor derelict in a cornfield. It is a cornfield where a straw man agrees with nature & not much has happened. We may assume that the straw man loves this tractor which some time ago yielded forty green tons per hour & now serves merely as a windbreak for the birds. The straw man is glad; he has been attacked from all sides throughout his life; it is better to toil here among the ravages than to live upon affections that will not penetrate the secret places of his woes. Even as the corn has lost its vigor, the quail come to him, a feast, though a feast that will expire. The straw man is only a stone's throw from the next town over, but he prefers the wherewithal of the once miraculous tractor, which allows for a future on his own terms. What will occur down the road is anyone's guess. It can be argued that the tractor will laugh last.

The Farm, 1922

Snowmelt feeds the eucalyptus, the
serifs of its leaves; feeds the farmer
who suffers like a condemned man; feeds
the hare, the uncompromising hare. The
hare is full of beans. The snail, the lizard,
the rooster, the goat exist on an even plane.
The hare emerges where it will. The
harlequin hare stands up to the moon.
The red tiles, the tin watering can, the
earthy earth make way for bare feet.
Here is the blizzard of the hare, which
the bean farmer has to weather when-
ever he is working the mundane field.

Caterpillar

Be gentle with the earth as you move it. You are a heavy lifter, articulate, inspiring the sluggish howitzer to blitz. That is, your traction takes tank to muck, truck to World War. And back. Boom to bust. Depression, a specialty, though in peacetime prosperity. Payload begins with appetite. The hungry caterpillar is natural – unnatural to children who step on it. For who is to say. That the earth is flat, that the CAT is yellow & black, that the hill is hell-bent. With a tree-line that must be leveled? Yes, you must regress if you are to establish the clear cut. The Waste Land has been ground to a pulp a million times over. It is no bed of roses. The velveteen sediment en route knows this. Wherever the machinations, voilà, a metamorphosis. Alas!

General Motors

Though the GM plant has long been abandoned, birches grow in its decaying heap of automotive manuals. Thus, after a generation of feeding, a grove arises, then papier-mâché automobiles, suspended in branches like nests. And the nobody who will never drive the automobiles also is summoned. Or perhaps he is somebody, a veritable Chief who paddles the Detroit River from Lake St. Clair. Yes, it is very clear that a sachem, Pontiac, is the driver of the birch-bark vehicles & that he foresees a floodplain full of headlights. Yes, it is very obvious that in the trees is an invention which Pontiac approves. The ideas of transmission, alternator, spoiler, & manifold can be sustained by trees; trees yield paper; paper yields Firebirds.

The Eunuch's Happy Vehicle

After a waltz through the parking lot,
the eunuch rejoices over his spangled
car. The car, for its part, is so attracted
to heaven that it feels uncomfortable.
Is smitten again. Some are born as
cars; some are made that way by
eunuchs. Some become cars for the
sake of the altogether lovely. Back in a
time when eunuchs were able to drive
wherever they wanted, the spangled
car tailed an earthbound taxi that left a
fervent place in its heart. Odd to think
of cars as having hearts, eunuchs as
having transport that might ferry
them to & above. Is there a mundane
essence that can be buried in heaven
like a spikenard? Where else can the
car go according to fragrant whims?

KELLOGG'S

The health nut takes a box of cornflakes to his grave. Good enough for the boy, good enough for the nostalgic, he says, leaning against the headstone, snacking, watching snow fall. And wistful for prizes. He is attached to those years; those years have a way with him; & the decoder ring just out of reach reminds him that the country graveyard, in which he lies, is no country at all, & yet, under the stars, the light is a homecoming. Light, at 186,000 miles-per-second, strikes the old guy who is now up to his neck in rimed flakes. Then the gentleman-farmer Mister Frost is fast upon him. Full of blank verse, he has something of consequence to say about what is & what is not in the cereal box.

HONEYWELL

Drones in the honeycomb sound off for war,
warfare, making the flower-children safe, safe to
criticize peacekeepers, who in their Pentagons like
a metronome give guidance, as well as technology
solutions gladsome & fearsome. All is well in the
hive when the monotone moans: peace, peace.
Even when there is no peace, no fair war, no
vouchsafe, the buzz is sticky, the hype is serious.
Going forth into aerospace, the mellow drones
repeat the golden rule: do unto others before
others do to you. That's more than the peace-
niks can say with Stingers aimed at themselves,
their own war chest, which is a hill to die on.

The Imperatives As They Occur

Piled on the white sands, pomegranates
& hand grenades. Who, what, why the
grenadiers, husbands of the desert, or
deserters? Who in his throwing motion
compels a pomegranate; what is the
fallout of desertion; why husband the
sands when nomads are through with
the fruit of their labors? Night on the
white sands, the cool white sands, the
lengths to which khaki silhouettes un-
fasten the pomegranates, grenades of
an antediluvian oasis, which is, shall be.

Dow

Evil can be explained by chemistry. For example, a fly swipes I-Can't-Believe-It's-Not-Butter from my bread. What sent it there, diseased, unwelcome? Chemicals. What's the solution? Pesticide. Tear gas is another fine invention. Why cry? Why else but for the woebegone fly that has escaped my lips, along with all the dirty words I've ever said because of atoms & all I've ever done for same. Agent Orange, Agent Orange, come in. Do you read me? I am at peace with Dow. The Tao of chemistry. Misbehavior made plain: the sniper in polypropylene, my chemical weapons. Neurotransmitters? Resins? These are reasons in & of themselves. I acknowledge a Law of Conservation. Nothing to be lost. Styrofoam goes into a landfill; saline causes a sea change for breasts. I can waste myself. Others.

KRAFT

Permit me to apply these squares of American cheese to my spacesuit. Is it that I am a man? Or crazed? How will such a man make it in space, the consuming fire of reentry, & the joy of it? I am a fat man. American. Vienna sausages have always been sweet music to my fingers, yet the Germanics have done so much damage. Except the rocketeers who engineered the success of the American space program. And it was the Germans who are half responsible for Ohio where Neil Armstrong was born. Could I advertise myself as a Kraft man, posting an American flag on the moon? Good question. Yes. But a better one might be: what kind of heat shield would American cheese provide? It's hard to believe that Ohio was once considered the Northwest Territory, that every small step West was a tap of the spacebar pitching us deeper into the shit. Frontiersmen wore leathers; what that did to their skin was barbaric. Yet Americans have come to occupy new worlds. Backspace←Shift↑Backspace←Shift↑

Fox

The traces of my fellow foxes, light-footed, quick-witted, are fugitive; you can find them, if you can find them, among Hawthorne's notebooks, though also in Aesop, foxes in their simpler states shrewd, telling tales out of school but, paradoxically, on the mark. The foxes in fables always move crooked; so says the fabulist. Which explains why movies were at first silent: the flick is foxfire, vixen. Who can tame the talkie? It seems a century ago (when a fox caught my tongue & dragged it to its den) that I was laid out on a La-Z-Boy. I got not a lick for my lazy bones.

Hornbook

They must give pleasure, rhinoceros &
hornbill, the horn of the rhino, the bird
with a nose for précis. Moonlight is
nosier than the hornbill whose probos-
cis is a curved thing, curved as a sickle.
At war or harvest, the sickle pleases.
It is a précis of cutlery, carving the
ambient noise, carving the ivory. The
darkness, in sum, is noisy with horns,
impeccable horns, horns of plenty.
Pointed as the noses are toward précis,
there is a raw verve in the night again.

Apple

You don't fall far from the tree. Is that because you are adamant? In Adam's fall/ we fell all, bruised? Software? What keeps us processing even if besotted? Knowledge? What's the big idea? Is it my soul in your interface? Me? Little i? My jot is a worm, my dot a wormhole. This hole attend/ my life to mend, for out of the chip the graphics grow? Or by trusting type, may I increase the font? No. The № 1 product of malfeasance is mindset. Folded. Blindfolded. "How do I know what I know?" I'm glad you asked; I'll get to that. Consider the letters, which serve the ready finding. They do not sow; they migrate. Yet always return to the same damn place. A is for Apple. No one has ever hated apple flesh. Touch, & touch again, the Corporation.

Remarkable Pears

Just to see how I will respond, the
technician paints an emu on my
belly. The emu is eating pears the
color of oxblood. The technician fills
out the tableau by adding an orchard
owned by no one in particular. Her
brush makes a trespass nevertheless.
The pears are like allegorical tumors
that the emu is only happy to rid me
of. Still, the fact that pears make an
appearance at all is disconcerting,
given the circumstances. This paint-
ing by the technician is becoming,
you might say, negative, except for the
emu. I'm grateful that the technician
has the foresight to start with it. The
emu is as graceful a flourish as there
is, though at this point I feel like I am
in a different place. I am increasingly
won over by the pears. They are easy
on the eyes, I confess, & to remove
them would seem like a violation.
What the technician is doing with her
hand, tracking the relative position of
emu to pears, pears to orchard, also is
persuasive. I remember the technician
saying, when this imaging began, I'd
have to be out of my mind to acquiesce.

PLAINTIVE

Neighbor, tell me a story, tell me of a
man & his ruthless flute, a ruthless
flute that plays little blue hornets. I
am afraid of hornets, but go on, say
something about the flautist, with
what virtue he plays, to what audi-
ence. I have waited off & on for a little
pep in my step, & if the hornets hurry
me along then let them do so. I could
stand for a suite of little blue hornets.
I'd wear that buzz wherever I would.
I'd say there was a man with a ruthless
flute & whatever is the matter, who
the hell are you, & why do you care.

What I Mean By Charles North

What I mean by Charles North is the
Charles River flowing in a northerly
direction, not for nothing, not a char-
latan nor a Charlemagne, not rueful.
North comes to me everywhere like
sailboats on the Charles; everywhere
it comes to me in barks tugged by a
Nor'easter. Easter is the holiday of
True North, a North to sally forth from,
a North to chart my forethoughts or
my aftermaths. This day a shipwright
like myself turns a lathe, turns to char-
ity, turns a tributary to the leeward.

The Ohio Element

To play the sonata in Toledo, I will
need a piano. And a peony in a vase
to set upon the grand. And a pair of
shears to snip the peony from the
garden, an Ashtabula garden where
rabbits levitate. And if necessary a
machine shop for the fabrication of
snips – of a similar temper as Chinese
scissors. I also require a scale to
weigh Youngstown steel, its heft. And
quicklime to address miscellaneous
slag. To delve into ore, as in aria, a
piano is not a rational instrument.
I would not be a genuine Ohioan
without the high-pitched rabbits.

The Sapient

When diagnosing diseases of the
brain, it's natural to think of grass-
fed, pasture-raised androids. The
androids on hands & knees do every-
thing involuntarily. If they love the
smell of irises in June, it is instinct-
ive. If they dream of a lawn that is
everlasting, it is behavioral, a kind of
Artificial Intelligence. They give the
turf how to & what for, but the glade
from which they spring is a garden
to which they are beholden. Caprice
or whim is second nature. After a
sip of scotch, a drag on a Nicaraguan
cigar, the pre-programmed husbands
leave the patio for den & flat screen.
It's beautiful to think of them as
hibernal, waiting in the truant light.

Calvin Klein

If there are sunspots on the male nude, & if in
the AM my own self-inspection, then meekly I
approach the familiar ape, meekly I shrink from the
spotlight. The freckled light, the blatant baboon. I
stare at myself in the bathroom mirror: why is it
that I am less when the light is voluptuous? A neon
Post-it note, stuck on glass, awakens me like Venus.
The hour has come to slip on ironed shirt, pinstripe
pants. There's a way to wear oneself in the world.

Dixon Ticonderoga

Leadhead rides the Express train into Emerald City, & I can understand why. The lost dog, the lost job, the lost wife. The loneliness of winter means a heavy trip to the zoo where the laughing gull makes a bullet of him. And so the fast train of tiger panels & leopard prints. I like the scenario where Leadhead pencils God in the heavens with coconut cream. The first question Leadhead ever asked was a giant propeller. The second had to do with a head of steam. Here lie the remains of Leadhead pretending to be monkish. In the quiet of a № 2 reverie, the temptation.

Red Cape, Yellow Mantle, Violet Tail, Blue Feet, Green Mouth

The perfect body does not seek a bird of paradise. On pace, the body rides ellipsis, the red carpet of ellipsis. The bird is an afterthought, a landing craft. A white astronaut steps out of the afterthought. Now that paradise has arrived, there is the sickness of infinitude. Wherein white astronaut. Wherein tether to dimensionless. It must be that an emissary of Los Angeles is both paradise & spacecraft. It cannot be that the candent starlet waves to the universe, steps lightly, disappears.

The Door To Ukulele

The metatarsal says to the door:
through you I step. The tibia & fibula
traipse after with loud shouts of accla-
mation, while the load-bearing spine,
like a forklift, rides serendipitously
over the threshold, for the door is
most certainly true. Looking back, the
cranium, whose tongue wagged as it
approached the lintel then entered,
gets its bell rung. What a bell it is that
swings between clavicles. The bell is
working hard, remembering where it
came from. It annunciates a different
movement than the trombone-playing
radius, which has struck up the band.
In the dark cave of the bell, not fear,
not rejoicing, but the whole shebang.

The Beats

The day the Earth stood still, imagi-
nation left us. There was a dead spot
on the lawn that we pretended was
not there. Under the flying saucer
of his hat, The Wizard of Ozone
Park announced it was springtime
& then, because he was vagabond,
took a footpath over the moon.
Wow! That's right! The newness
was barely new. We said yeah to rub-
bing our neighbor's pussy willows,
wands that would never ever be ours.

The Body Shop

This is my body, an idyllic corporation. To my
devotees, I sell vanities. There are heavenly
bodies; there are terrestrial bodies. The splendor
of one exceeds the other, especially on the sixth
day when manicured Adam, pedicured Eve, wade
neck deep in libations. This Eden can be tender
as a chemical peel that exfoliates, disappears with
unguents. I love the ways my ass has been caressed
& from so many directions. I think it was a word
that inspired me to believe that a body, dead &
buried, is a means to the imperishable. Is it for that
reason I to my bedfellows whisper sweet nothings?

The Sidereal Messenger

Because death has no power over him, the astronomer waits at the bottom of a river. Lucifer above him, though tempted to strafe, tips his wings according to bylaws. At the riverside, the screech of birds. A jaguar leaves them alone; what for? It is said that the eating of peacocks is verboten & the headhunting tradition has gone dark. Love is coming in the searchlight that creeps. The star man does not know what day it is, does not yet sense the invisible quark nor the boson that will bless, does not intuit the moons of Jupiter, their snow hearts. What he sees is the sweetgum as it bends over the broad river, leaves that fret. If he is to deliver news, good news, he will first have to fail at being the epicenter of things.

THE CONSUMER

The Wilderness After Which

We went back to our quiet lives, &
displaying our marigold spirit we
prepared for the strangers that would
inhabit Cape Cod. Look at us in our
handsome waistcoats, they said as
they arrived, graybeards with ruffled
collars. They came to us, green
around the gills, plying a Mayfair
speech. They came with coins in
their mouths, albeit professing a
windblown currency. Thousands
were fed when they disproportioned
their skin & bones. The strangers
fished around & told us of ourselves,
we as we once were, we as we are still.

The Angler

The fisherman in this anecdote is in love with the indefinite article, which is like unto a fish, a notorious fish that is said to live omnisciently in the headwaters. The fish, often remarked upon but rarely engaged, has words with the angler, rainbow words on a cloudy day. What passes between them is authentic local color, but understood is that there are other stippled beauties not of these parts. Where to cast, then? What lure? How far?

THE THROWER

I killed a man with a javelin. The javelin wobbled in the air but made no sound. The victim was a gray man in a flannel suit, & the javelin went through him. I did not heave the way I wanted to heave. I let go without the foggiest idea of who he was. He lay in the grass like a banker just returned from the vault. The javelin was made of rare earth metals; the financier was mostly a composite. He seemed to me all that is best & worst of Wall Street. There, a man may cry out while unbuttoning his shirt, exposing his ample bosom.

Barker

I saw you under the fig tree picking
up fruit then sampling it. You had
been at a carnival; you had been on
a unicycle wheeling through the
desert when the figs looked up at
you with sumptuous lips, thereby
arresting your momentum. You were
astounded that what they said was so
agreeable. The shapeliness of their
prosody appealed to the connoisseur
in you. That the figs must have had
suitors, you were well aware. You
smuggled them into your knapsack
lest the vesper bats & golden jackals
have their way with them. Now that
you teeter before me, rich in flesh,
you must decide if you can leave their
sweets behind & stick to my bones.

Hallmark

Call in an air strike so that the heart might feel
something. Let the heart be greeted in giftwrap &
fellow feeling. Thick muscle, hard of hearing: the
heart that lost friends, comrades, mute comrades.
Their silence purchased with keepsakes, canards.
Go and catch a falling star. Let skylarks sing their un-
premeditated art; the heart cares more or less. Give
it a rest; sympathize with the hack. To U.S., the one
thing onerous is a sentiment no one understands.

CHASE

Or be chased. This is a law of nature, as witnessed in salmon that run. From bear. Or bull. Whatever the market, pursue your course. It won't be long; nothing's for certain. I can see the futures, if successful, are billions. They satisfy a fiduciary obligation which, whether self-imposed or government-regulated, contributes to streams; gold is a good color for the glitter of your back & forth. The other day, in mid-sentence, I held current. I was the environment asking for the unreal; I wanted to know if there was sanctuary in the affluent through which you passed. It had next to nothing to do with securities, derivatives, bondage.

Big Sur

Let's take a Vespa to the beach; let's
not get killed. Our lives are mir-
rors, adjust your mirrors, let's not
get killed. The sun goes over a cliff,
head over heels. We motor away—
switchback. Us versus the sun—
vice versa, we're golden. Let's take a
Vespa to the beach; let's not get killed.

PLUTOCRATS

Plutocrats, once fragrant with the green of spring, are hoarding lightning. Then why hearts with black spots leaping, why, in the blight of autumn, do leaves have seven eyes? Do leaves have seven eyes? I think they might be autumnal; I think they might be lightening the heavy nights & the hoarfrost which was, is, is to come. When blighted hearts leap, chartreuse as grasshoppers, the eyes will, with heavy nights, ransom the earth, as plutocrats give up their wanton hordes: flies, lightning in a bottle.

David Foster Wallace

Outside the Frost Library, the butter-
flies have been exterminated. If you
let me into the library, I will get some
Frost. I will get woods, pastures, a
conversation to brook. The Monarchs
in field guides disregard my high
sentences. They make me feel like a
snowman with Hairstreaks. I blurt
out something orotund in my note-
book about ∞. How could I know the
height, the depth, of that floating fact?

DOLE

You know me; you know where I am headed. I shill in the aisles of the supermarket. No watchman will keep my lips from premium Bartlett pears, no kill-joy will block my way to the orchard that fortifies within the can. There is beatitude on the faces of consumers; I feed them pomes in gold streaks. I mean to say that labels are for the eyes of the lucid, whereas the tongue is utterly brazen. I gloss, guilt-free, my cornucopian perishables. Here: have a pear.

JOHNSON & JOHNSON

The shampoo bottle became a projectile. It performed three touch-and-go landings before departing the airspace of the peninsula. The NO MORE TEARS, in its plastic rocket, cartwheeled out over the Pacific. No one knew the sentiments of the shampoo as it sloshed in the bottle. Nor, when it disappeared into the dolorous waves, was anyone able to uncap it. Down it went the throat of the ocean & left no afterword, no sound signature, though in its heyday it had inspired so many of the harebrained to sing along.

FORD

If it's all the same to you, I'd like something more than horsepower. In the '70s, I listened to service tips from a Ford dealer on the radio; it made me eager to own a Thunderbird, or lose the past in a Galaxie. But when push came to shove, it was a Mazda, Japanese-assembled. Fast-forward to the future, to the yachts of Grand Traverse where Chicagoans from the Gold Coast are insane for our lakefronts. It's true that the high & mighty are mired in foreclosure. You got to feel for the jet set. That puts me in mind of high school when Led Zeppelin ruled the airwaves. Transport is fickle. One of the first Fords, the 999, shot across ice like an Arrow but also killed its test-driver. Glaciers; they tiptoed interstate with nary an engine.

Small Machines Made of Words

They were, they are, they will be
Lepidoptera. They fly in pirouettes
& exaggerations. What have they to
do with hands that may or may not
be praying? Their resting place is in
the fluvial beard of the typesetter. In
concert with the typesetter, the beard
crosses the Brooklyn Bridge, taking
the folded wings with it. The butter-
flies are Metalmarks that match the
girders of the Brooklyn. Of what font
is the river, upsetting the typesetter,
carrying his typeface into harangues &
later meeting up with the bookbinder?
For whom is the crisscross if not for
commuters in their prosaic costumes?

Big Shot

The prospect of the bear with stars
on her body, light exiting the body at
breathtaking speed, lopes before him.
The excited animal begins to play in the
mind – strange how the unemployed
so far have overlooked her. They lack
business sense, a certain *je ne sais quoi*.
But the executive tilts his head upward.
He targets the bear repeatedly with his
telescope & crunches the numbers.
How much margin realistically can
he clear on ursine packages of gravity,
color, & plasma? On the dry-erase
board he writes: I do not know how I
come across to the astronauts, but to
myself I have always been an adventurer.

The Insomniac

On second thought, the merchants
will not open. I like it best, or better,
when the merchants open, for the
hollow in their throats is the same
as, not different than, the hollow in
my backyard after shoveling, a long
night of hacking & pitching. Stripped
to the waist, it is almost as if I am a
gravedigger laying the green turf on
the pan of my spade, which is an
open tool unlike a hammer. I think
the merchants would become vulner-
able if I took a hammer to their plate
glass. Why is it that I hold a shovel
when a hammer will do just as well,
or why is it that I swipe their card
processors rather than love letters?
The night deserves a talking-to; I have
so much to say to the merchants who
keep from me their funny business.

Lost Dialect

I wish to be alive under my hat, &
mouth off like a crow, a blue-eyed black-
bird in a sequoia. I would speak my
mind to other crows, crowds in a blue
sky. Knowing that each creature has
its own ideas, I would let my fellows
cache their theories & fake cache.
And when one crow to my own throes
would succumb, I would surround it,
then leave silently on my way to the
database, crownless in a data cloud.

ORIGINAL MULE

The river waits for the monologue of
a pink tongue. The darkness is fetch-
ing. It invites sightseeing, though
there is a decided absence of moon-
light. As the tongue approaches, what
does it see? Does it see opaquely that
there are coal-fire power plants & a
night of star anise, oblong barges & a
myrrh sunrise? The tongue ventures
out into sepia vapors where a mule
flicks extravagant ears & conifers
along the sable river char. How could
we not want the mule, the original
mule cut whole cloth out of feeling?
It sashays decoratively in a stride that
will not be parsed among exuberant
leaves. The fashionable ass shifts
its burden, happier in work than we
tired tailors deserve; whatever whim
is felt has survived our nimble shears.

FALSE COW

The guardian of dim clouds, how long did he live in Iowa? How far did he drive the false cow, did he take it to the red city? Was there a commotion of the elements? Was there a pasture where the animal laid its head? Did the cow have a smooth brain, was it a cow of many ways? Were the clouds symphonic? Was the falsehood serene, did it wear a crown of thorns, did it talk to itself while goring others? When he arrived in the red city with a switch, might the guardian have been culpable? Did the lights go on, albeit dimly? What of the lodestones that rained down from the clouds, how were they received, to whom were they intended? Would the Iowans harried by irons put on their suits of magnetic stripes? Would they busk outside of shops to beg their bread? Would they sing out, mendicants of the pastures, for the divine right to discombobulate?

McDonald's

Old McDonald had a farm. And the rest of us
bought the farm, but having bought it, what to
do? What's done is done; did a number on us;
why? Not that special sauce is patently formulaic,
just that stock isn't what it used to be. Nature has
a beef with it: how to package it. Ever so piqued,
our sacred cow, parsed, secretly spiced. Out of
the fryer, the recombinant body parts; what next?
Each day, another additive: ee-i-ee-i-o. Okay.
Granted. But on that farm a flavor that makes
the tongue taste better, enhanced. We go hog
wild over it. The money will take care of itself.

The God Bug

Out of a green encumbrance, the
god bug flies. Fly away, uninvited
deity. I do not understand you. Nor
the Persian cat in the lap of a
turnip field. Nor why I am hitting
Jim Crow with a tobacco stick. Nor
how the stick flowers. The god bug
amazes the farm, days without end.
If conditions are sour for turnips, no
matter. When tobacco is uncured in
the rafters, what is that to providence?
I remember, after striking him, Jim
Crow coming at me with a pistol. In
a catastrophe, there is nothing left
of time. The bullet dallies; the pistol
repeats what the Persian mews. Jim
Crow lives on my property. He lights
the fire in my kitchen; we exchange
words. He is intoxicated, as all men
are when toiling in a green encum-
brance. I do not understand the
turnip, the way it ripens red & purple
wherever the sun has fallen. Nor the
peevishness of the revolver as I brave
Jim Crow & the confederacy I deny.

True Value

Hands flex to resist the hostile advances of the steel rake. The possum is half-human. It feels; it wants to live. Lying on its back, it gingerly accepts the tines as fingers of an alien, the way babies do when probed. Docile piece of aluminum, the possum. It smiles at the rake's weird teeth.

The Golden Days of Textiles

Someone has made you a shirt, what wonderful news. Wrinkle-free, you lie in it & fall asleep. The night you perceive as displacing you follows suit, lets go of the preoccupations that came to pass & is flattened & guided into sleeves. The emaciated arms, the open neck, reveal a casualty. I hate war, said Lorca, or could have, while ghostwriting of a time hence, a time of great guile when the you of the future would earn a wage, embellishing. And the fabrications you indulge now for something other than money are reflected in these tortoiseshell buttons that someone has applied, buttons that you finger in the same way you finger sun & moon, your shirttail untucked, the noonday anon upon you.

Time Signature For
Sapphire Tuba

Once you get over the panic, there
is the blue suit & a deep voice out of
cadence. The deep voice hears itself
out of step with the world, fearful,
running from white noise. It is a
good thing that the blue suit stays
the course. It is a blood thing that a
scarlet ibis approaches the fogged
windows of your house. The ibis
leads a life very different from yours.
You are at home in the blue suit,
with the silk knot of a deep voice
loosened, ready to turn a blind eye.

The Sublime Hiss

Icebergs have visited Florida, so it is time for a chisel. What a kick to drag blocks to your icehouse & with calipers to stack them. Perhaps the anhinga will help you address the ice; the man-of-war that confronts you also will help you. A palm tree ruffles your feathers, yet for other reasons you are a sculptor. Given its proximity to the equator, the icehouse is less icehouse. You have heard me say that the clearest bluest berg yields the best ice. I know you well, friend. You think about offering but refuse me a glass of cold water.

The Station

The oceanographer was sent to a station in the middle of the woods, & I am informed he was my father, yes, he was my Abba to whom I beckon, he with his headphones listening to sine waves, emanations from a great distance, & around him the owls voicing their opinions politely. Those days in the woods, & nights, swallowing the murmurs as they whelmed, trained him in the art of concentration. The owls were his retinue. I was pleasantly surprised when they told me how intimate he could be with the waves.

Amazon

Cry me a river so I can ship to domestics my
far-flung packets, parcels scarcely considered,
embarked on episodes advantageous, though
contrary to custom, contraband smartly pursued,
for a time waylaid then tracked across Americas,
conveniences that make the good life better. A
Pony Express can run fast enough, even with
broken legs, but a river blazes its own trail without
footfall or hobble & makes headway over hill/dale
because it's fleeting, or, to use another electric
phrase, hot to trot. The curios flow, Trade-winds
blow, the tributary bends; bendable = expendable,
& that's one more boon for commerce. Epicurean
to excess, the empty box-catchers, yet quick
to American Express their fancy for the wide-
spread because they must answer their wishes
when hungry; satisfaction is provisional albeit
guaranteed. I have failed to mention the pygmies.
NEXT-DAY, HOLIDAY, OVERNIGHT: will send promptly.

NIKE

The clouds, black with the night, are winded, perpetually winded. A woman in a business suit crawls across the lake, & she's not a bush pilot, though the interior is dark & it seems as if she's discovering resources. And she's not a mountaineer, though she traverses. The crevasse of the journey cannot keep the woman from the other side. The distance is deceptive, as is the detachment with which she dips ungloved hands like spoons into coffee. Because the lake is stimulant; because the Corporation wants only her.

THE CITY

THE CITY, 1912

The rabbit with human hands fashions a human city. I have been to that metropolis; it is a city of carrots & squashes. It emits a definite shade of red & a yellow undertone. The huntsman bivouacs on its outskirts. There is another city not far off & not made with human hands. In its tower, a violet bell. The violet bell strikes a velvet sound; it rings a definite shade of maybe. The violet bell cannot be dulled. It quivers in the hands implausibly. Wherever the soft, deep colors go round, the huntsman traipses. The possible rabbit with the impossible extremes is sometimes near, sometimes loose. It circles back to where the huntsman lapses. There is no must in the violet city; the humane rabbit is free to make again.

General Electric

Whether by daylight, candlelight, or light-emitting diode, we laugh at the colorful. We capture in a field the NBC peacock, the world's most chromatic bird. And the most acrimonious because light is upon it. Said peacock is not sanguine that we catch it by the tail, that we are pulling its leg, that we are roasting it over a bed of bedazzlement. (Shades of the Dark Ages). Watching it unsparingly, we render it unsavory – unseasonable – better dead than alive. As in Rembrandt's *Bittern*, which the artist found posed in the reeds, mottled & barred, a likeness that today appears lackluster whenever the Internet of Things copies it. The coy bird, ambivalent about the Dutchman's moods (his tints, his hallmarks), quails at the portraiture. Imagine that.

PepsiCo

When you, like a billion others, watch sunflowers in
a field, how easy to say they are fervent. There are
powder burns on their faces; there are heat waves in
which they let themselves go, leading to altercations.
Under the blistering sky where you linger, a vague
sense of overkill, so vague you speak out of turn.
The man from Pepsi Cola has been all afternoon
among the flowers distributing sodas in his red,
white, & blue. You don't mean to be ungrateful for
the Pepsi man, the jangle of quarters, the carbon-
ated sibilants of whistles being wetted. But you can't
help but agitate for something else, for the man
to pull out of his pocket an invoice from which he
will read figures, an impromptu reading that will
force him to don riot gear & hold up a night stick,
as sunflowers turn to listen, & rave up & down.

The Censor

The censor goes to work on a cigar; he
puts the head in a guillotine & removes
the cap; he is toasting the foot with a
blue flame; smoke draws through the
barrel; he tastes the wrapper; before
him is a short story, a Hemingway;
the censor is in A Clean, Well-lighted
Place; he is wearing a linen shirt; his
fingers roll the offending onionskin
into a Corona; the keys are definitely
hitting the ribbon like hard, hard
rain; he is perspiring; the ash at
the end of the cigar maintains its
perfect cylindrical shape; he blacks out
rectangles of text with capital Xs; a fan
is blowing; parakeets fly awkwardly in a
cage; they are billowing their wings; the
moon is up to this point an imaginary
sphere where the birds do not belong,
yet moonward they pretend; there's
something in the palimpsest the censor
must address; he retrieves a № 2
pencil & a sheaf of snow-white paper
where he can mass-produce the effect.

The Martyr's Merry
Cherry Bomb

I am writing to you on account of the
Metropolitan, whose head smolders,
there being a fuse on top that is lit
from without. You may find it hard to
believe that nothing sets it off since
the head bangs with laughter, the mob
incensed. There is no reason, however,
for uproar. In martyrdom, any guffaw
if pure is also intrinsically volatile, for
each breath causes a numinous vibra-
tion. It is clear that all I have said thus
far of the Metropolitan is provisional,
& so are the concussions. Perhaps
with envy & a mournful sympathy we
respect them. Certainly, each burst
will find expression in zeal, but there
will always be something left over that
zeal fails to express & that yet is not
ambrosial. Not only repulsion makes up
this ambivalence but private qualms of
which how could we know? The hilarity
of the cherry bomb nonetheless acts
as a welcome pulse in the turmoil of
our inner life. We hear in it a ceasefire
or an armistice from a forgotten age.

UNITED

At each other's throats, the artificers; yet I want
to say they conspired in the stratosphere. I want
to ask: who might be there to receive them but
the Dreamliner, new to the fleet? At logger-
heads, the uncivil engineers drew up plans for
a mile-high city; without altimeters, they aimed
to disappear into thin air. They bickered. And
as they bickered, they assembled themselves
with guy-wires & propellers for a maiden flight.
The artificers spent an eternity devising simply
because the skies were determined to be friendly.

LACHRYMOSE

It is, of course, possible that the
umbrella stand in the basilica, where
the umbrellas pause as if awestruck,
is evidence of a theophany; that the
stranded tourists tote the umbrellas
to ward off the Man of Sorrows; that
while the tourists sit in pews, thor-
oughly saturated, the verboten sky has
had a change of heart & the wayfarers
whose names have been cut & pasted
on manifests will be lifted up imper-
ceptibly into the atmosphere; that
they riffle through the bulletins in the
alcove in order to kill time, then fold
them into accordions which, like the
vaulted heavens, stifle violent sobs.

GOODWILL

Here is a barn. I toss my hate in the loft & walk away. The hate that once warmed my head stays put while I wander elsewhere. When I die, the feeling remains. Here is a boy. He enters the barn & discovers my unseemly habit. The hate now holds his head. At school, he is known for it. His mother can't get him to take it off during supper; in her day, failure to remove one's hate was a punishable offense. Fortunately, the boy outgrows it. Even if he could still brandish the hate, he wouldn't. It is no longer a trademark. Wit is what makes him stand out. Classmates smart weeks after his gibes of petty amusement. Seeing the uselessness of the headwear, the mother donates it to a thrift store.

Goodyear

It was a good year, a bad year, a year without end.
There was wasteland, odyssey, war. It mattered
that those who manufactured bounced back, made
up ground. Oh the places they would go where no
human race is! Hysteria, inflation, hot air – what the
thunder said was better said by engines, airships.
The zeitgeist got into zeppelins that went around
the world, upside down, belly up. Lord, the thunder
cried, even these speech balloons are breathtaking.

Discover

The universe, what do we know about it? Some of us claim to have been there, to have come from there. But can we define what it is we have sought without forgery? There is a somewhere wherever we have arrived, brand new, as good as new. Do we love the nirvana that novelty has bought? Replicated, all of us, many of us counterfeit, having never discovered a place for the genuine & therefore unable to identify. We were hatched. How strange it was to be alive.

The Snow Pyramid

You look out at the snow pyramid. It is lit by a streetlight & has followed you home. You relax in a chair embroidered with tigers; the snow pyramid is imperious. You change the light in your study to a mercury bulb; the darkness outside the house interprets. You know what you know; the snow goes about its business. You quiet yourself; you think about the manager who came to embalm you on this the first day of the week. Insofar as you are making money hand-over-fist, you begin to imagine a scheme. The pyramid is nowhere to be found. The alarm rings. Time to live.

If Rightly The Virgin Is Called

The cruiser swiftly appears. On the dash is a radar gun that, with the hand of the Deputy, brings the State of Virginia to bear. And the Virgin, Holy Mother of God, emerges from the back of the squad car while we, in the van in front of the cruiser & its blue flashing lights, cry "Innocent!" When climbing out of our vehicle, keeping our hands where the Officer can see them, we step onto cinders along the berm. We pay little attention to the Deputy's chevrons, for we ourselves are newly uniformed attendants. The six-winged seraphim make perfect sense, as does the doubtful gryphon. The stars that look out from the benighted squad car ice the heart contusions we have nursed from birth.

The Revelation Of St. Robot

It's almost as if they had the obituary
ready to go, but he refreshed. He must
have felt that it was his job to keep
himself alive. He sat in the back room
morning after morning & waited for
the usual horseshit. It showed up
when the sun was traffic-light green.
I liked what St. Robot said, even the
way he said it, but after a while I grew
tired of it. Who was here? Someone,
obviously, since these are his things.
At some point, however, he must
have evacuated. To translate, I think.

Marathon

The marathoner runs flat-footed in a no-man's land enthused with a panegyric. In the thick of the race, she loses sight, does not falter, takes heart. It is a most ancient heart that leaves her breathless. When in doubt, she goes West. No, she does not suffer her paean to be enslaved. Nor, panting, has she lost the American spirit, which is as winsome as it is a win-win proposition. The land that is no man's lies. As if possessed. The marathoner runs on pain-killers to the end of her pace, paying no heed, going the distance, doling out praise. Hark the herald who is strident.

TOMATILLO

I talk as if I know of what I speak.
I act as if I have the wherewithal to
cross the Great Lake with only the
lantern of a tomatillo. That would be
bizarre, trusting in a green light. A
starless expanse, the wreck of a canoe,
a tomatillo warm from my garden.
The day that was long lives longer in
the nightshade. The beetle goes on
unseen, consumed with luxurious
eating. I can't, at the taciturn moon,
be outraged. I discover a soft spot
which looks like blight but is light.

The Hunger

The gun, in the crook of the bishop's arm, does not belong here. The knife that has been trained to slaughter rabbits also is a misfit. Bullets in the bishop's sex organs make waves. The fly that torments the bishop's head ignites him. An airplane alone is true to the skies above the Mediterranean Sea where boats skim for sardines. Smoke from the bishop's pipe floats over the almond trees; seagulls fight over the spines of the fish, which languish on campfires. The seers of Catalonia brandish rainbows above the horizon. A sentimental hunger propels the bishop's stiff legs toward salted cod & cold beer.

Disclosure

The red farmhouse, on a rood or
two of garden-ground near the sea
where mariners harbor and blue-
jackets disperse, at one time found the
morning light; chilled & benumbed
the light whenever a phoebe nesting in
the rafters poked its fly-catching head
out, aware that the household could
momentarily burst into wide, genial,
comprehending silences, hence the
infinite fraternity of feeling that
persuaded the rest of us that the farm-
house in letters & correspondences
was a scarlet book in which, shame-
less, we malingerers capaciously read.

Whereabouts

Hopper would have loved this light
hitting the clapboard. As he entered
the canvas with a brush, Hopper
would have worked quietly & waited
for the man in an ultramarine suit
who would have driven up to the
clapboard house in a convertible.
The man would have come from
the seaside carrying a briefcase. The
man's name would have been Strand,
as in stranded for a long time, as in
castaway. Strand would have stepped
out of the car & approached the house
via the mackerel walkway provided by
Hopper. There would have been a line
of dunes, burnt grass, & a penumbra
where Hopper would have settled
in to watch a lackadaisical sail pass
behind the house & then annihilate it.

Incessant Bird Revealing
The Unknown

Seemingly out of the blue, a birdwatcher
throws stones. The cuckoo is petrified
because the birdwatcher is a neighbor;
never before has any unpleasantness
passed between them. Then also the
birdwatcher is impeccably dressed.
Such a warden is unimpeachable,
God be praised! The fey woodland, the
twilight decrepitude are improvised.
The gravitas of the birdwatcher is upset
by this recent breach of decorum. The
cuckoo, nested as it is in the storybook
forest, is having a real hard time of it.

Night Is Hapless
Rabbit Is Lippy

When the dreamer tires of decomposing, is it nothing to discover a pelt where there is vehement rabbit? No less carcass, the moon sheds light on amnesty, including the warm body where the ardent rabbit tabernacles. The cows that twinkle-toe in the asters are hardly worth mentioning, except to suppose they venerate, well-pleased.

Black Swans

What of the black swans that swim
in ice melt? Where have they gone?
Where can we find them? Could we
take if we wanted the silver glide path?
They might be at the end of it, where-
as we would start out lighthearted.
Dark matter would surprise us. Also
momentum, the argentine in their
wake as chimeric as arriving. Might
we dream up another scenario, one
where, insatiable for light, the swans
become full of themselves, vacuum-
ing stardust out of the microcosm,
after which they would apologize,
making us sympathizers, the likes
of which we would barely recognize?

MYSTIC HORSE

Once a millennium, a unicorn comes
along, white shadow of fantastical
things. To think that you befriend the
myth at risk of being censored! You
take note of its whims & pin them
to your jacket until you are a tapes-
try of the incredulous. When you
return home, tired but elated, your
spouse hangs up your coat, unpins
the scraps of paper, & lays them on
the desk for you to piece together.
Before you the memoranda but also
the sad rumor of hush money that
makes the unicorn essential. You
have no choice but to enthusiastically
speak since Earth itself permits chaos
& how else might you beautify save
with rampage? You are willing to en-
dure a horn that grows between eyes.

The Iron Ewe

She's out of your grasp. She moves
among idle thoughts but won't linger.
She refuses to be aroused. This morn-
ing I noticed you ruling her with an
iron fist. An ordinary ewe might wilt
under the circumstances, but this
one is impervious. She looks to be
genuinely steadfast outside the fold.
You cannot unnerve her; you are too
embarrassed to ask for help. Seems
your days of wool-gathering are over.
You carry electric tape to shut her trap
& copper wire to galvanize her. You
hope for the best. The iron ewe does
what no other ewe can. Why won't
she, when you ask her so nicely?

The Overcoat

Now the woman in the overcoat, a top coat teeming with locusts, is meadow bound. She wears the twitching wings through the lobby of the Time-Life building. And I am an employee separated from my swarm; what is the fastest way to the meadow that I might retrieve the overcoat, which she must have found hooked on the door to my office? The eyes of the locusts are upon me while the woman pulls them close to her. It may be the coldest day of the year – that's what the temperature said – but if I am to propagate I will need their red eyes looking elsewhere. With the bent key to the Time-Life in my pocket, I spill out of the revolving door. The glare of the woman catches me in traffic. As I call out to the overcoat, mouths come apart at the seams.

Yahoo

What are we doing handcuffed behind our backs &
forced to walk on water? The horned ears of the owl
seem like quotation marks borrowed from a book,
empty of query, or are we the interlocutors? Our
hands are frozen, & yet we fold them; our feet are
stones to steal our thunder. The snow has made us
pure, almost blind, perhaps invisible. All winter, the
owl has been after us. We are no Oracle. How can we
say in machine language what it has already said?

Penguin

Fog subsumes the iceberg, an intermittent peak the
only signal, & whosoever wishes to write also leaves
a beauty mark on the white space of the horizon.
The mark will be a cartouche; within the cartouche,
a penguin. May it impart to the vapor a loopy eye of
watchfulness, as if to confirm that, in the middle of
nowhere, here is a living thing. Let us ask of that
eye, as of the absent iceberg, a belief in archipelago;
let us begin yet again in the barren incunabula.

Utmost Leopard

Friends of the leopard on the white
path regard the leopard as inescap-
able. The aforesaid makes a beeline
that is approximate to a leap. It con-
cerns all involved that the leopard
materializes wherever it wants in the
time it wants. Outside the window,
where the white path is not white but
merely nothing, the big cat has a field
day. A hunter, in a field of sable, tracks
the sun in order to parse the spots last
sighted. It can be heard & wondered
at that the leopard changes its spots,
but it cannot be certain. There is a
guardrail wherein the spotlight stops;
as if to say that the leopard, sufficient
in itself, contains itself. The way
they saunter, the friends might lope
or lie down beside the white path.
Now, now not, the leopard is slow
to speak but on a murderous pace.

NOTES

"Starbucks" borrows, recycles, or modifies language from Herman Melville's *Moby Dick*; "Deere" from Henry David Thoreau's *Walden*; "The Eunuch's Happy Vehicle" from Matthew 19:12 and the sermons of Charles Spurgeon; "Honeywell" from Jeremiah 6:14 and Luke 6:31; "Fox" from G. K. Chesterton's introduction to *Aesop's Fables*; "Apple" from the *New England Primer*; "The Body Shop" from 1 Corinthians 15; "The Sidereal Messenger" from the title of an astronomical treatise published by Galileo in 1610; "Barker" from John 1:48; "Hallmark" from John Donne's "Song: Go and catch a falling star" and Percy Bysshe Shelley's "To a Skylark"; "Small Machines Made of Words" from William Carlos Williams's introduction to "The Wedge"; "Big Shot" from a line attributed to Isaac Newton; "False Cow" from Dante's *Inferno*; "Disclosure" from Nathaniel Hawthorne's notebooks, gleaned out of Paul Auster's *Twenty Days with Julian & Little Bunny by Papa*; "The City, 1912" from Wassily Kandinsky's 1912 essay "Concerning the Spiritual in Art" and from Marcel Proust's *Remembrances of Things Past*; "Goodyear" from familiar lines of Robert Frost, T. S. Eliot, and Dr. Seuss; "The Hunger" from Joan Miró's diagrammatic notes to his 1923 painting "The Hunter (Catalan Landscape)"; "Incessant Bird Revealing The Unknown" from the title of Joan Miró's 1941 work "The Beautiful Bird Revealing The Unknown To A Pair Of Lovers (Constellation Series)"; "Mystic Horse" from a story told by George Marsden about Jonathan Edwards in *Jonathan Edwards: A Life*.

"The Tractor" reacts to a passage in Wendell Berry's Jefferson Lecture, "It All Turns on Affection": "We should, as our culture has warned us over and over again, give our affections to things that are true, just, and beautiful. When we give our affection to things that are destructive, we are wrong. A large machine in a large, toxic, eroded cornfield is not, properly speaking, an object or a sign of affection."

"The Farm, 1922" engages Joan Miró's painting of that name, as well as his 1927 work "Landscape (The Hare)."

"General Motors" responds to Andrew Moore's collection of photographs, *Detroit Disassembled*.

"What I Mean By Charles North" invokes, among other things, the American poet, Charles North, b. 1941.

"The Ohio Element" is derived obliquely from a passage in the Wallace Stevens essay "The Irrational Element In Poetry." "If I dropped into a gallery I found that I had no interest in what I saw. The air was charged with anxieties and tensions. To look at pictures there was the same thing as to play the piano in Madrid this afternoon."

"The Angler" is dedicated to my colleague, Bill Vande Kopple, who was an avid fisherman, grammarian, and reader of Gerard Manley Hopkins.

"Remarkable Pears" and "Dole" grow out of, and afield from, the "Theft of the Pears" chapter in Augustine's *Confessions*.

"The Station" is enthused by an anecdote novelist Kazuo Ishiguro tells in an interview with Susan Hunnewell in *The Paris Review, The Art of Fiction No. 196*.

"If Rightly The Virgin Is Called" reconfigures William Blake's 1823 pen and ink watercolor "Beatrice Addressing Dante from the Car."

"The Revelation of St. Robot" emerges, in part, out of Charles Simic's interview with James Tate in *The Paris Review, The Art of Poetry No. 92*.

"Whereabouts" elegizes American painter Edward Hopper and American poet Mark Strand.

Several poems from the collection take their titles from, and are inspired by, the names of American corporations. "The Body Shop" and "Penguin," though British and not U.S. companies, have been active in American business for decades.

ACKNOWLEDGMENTS

The author gratefully acknowledges the following magazines in which poems from the book first appeared:

STARBUCKS, DOW, APPLE, KRAFT, KELLOGG'S, THE OHIO ELEMENT, GOODWILL, TOMATILLO, AND DAVID FOSTER WALLACE in *The Common*;
THE SNOW PYRAMID, PEPSICO, NIGHT IS HAPLESS RABBIT IS LIPPY, and CATERPILLAR in *Crazyhorse*;
SMALL MACHINES MADE OF WORDS, THE CENSOR, and WHEREABOUTS in *Denver Quarterly*;
GENERAL MOTORS in *The Michigan Poet*;
FORD in *Poetry in Michigan/Michigan in Poetry*;
DOLE and JOHNSON & JOHNSON in *Eleven Eleven*;
CHASE, HALLMARK, DEERE, YAHOO, and NIKE in *Drunken Boat*;
AMAZON in *Mississippi Review*;
THE THROWER in *The Curator*;
THE CITY, 1912 and UTMOST LEOPARD in DIAGRAM;
ORIGINAL MULE and LOST DIALECT in *Copper Nickel*;
THE INSOMNIAC and THE WILDERNESS AFTER WHICH in *Ghost Town*;
THE HUNGER in *Wag's Revue*;
THE SAPIENT and IF RIGHTLY THE VIRGIN IS CALLED in *Salt Hill*;
THE OVERCOAT in *Fourteen Hills*;
PLUTOCRATS in *Phoebe*;
RED CAPE, YELLOW MANTLE, VIOLET TAIL, BLUE FEET, GREEN MOUTH and PLAINTIVE in *The Great American Literary Magazine*;
THE TRACTOR in *Michigan Quarterly Review*;
FALSE COW and THE FARM, 1922 in *Ladowich Magazine*;
THE EUNUCH'S HAPPY VEHICLE in *Colorado Review*;
GOODYEAR, HONEYWELL, PENGUIN, and FOX in *Carolina Quarterly*;
BIG SHOT in *Birmingham Poetry Review*;
TIME SIGNATURE FOR SAPPHIRE TUBA in *32 Poems*;
DIXON TICONDEROGA in *Hayden's Ferry Review*;
THE SIDEREAL MESSENGER in *Sycamore Review*;
BIG SUR in *Gulf Coast*

The author also would like to express gratitude to *Poetry Daily* and *Verse Daily* for reprinting some of these poems and for their generous, ongoing service to the art.

Special thanks to Guy Bennett, Paul Vangelisti, Esther Lee and the editorial team at Otis Books | Seismicity Editions.

Hélène Sanguinetti, *Hence This Cradle*
Janet Sarbanes, *Army of One*
Severo Sarduy, *Beach Birds*
Adriano Spatola, *The Porthole*
———, *Toward Total Poetry*
Carol Treadwell, *Spots and Trouble Spots*
Paul Vangelisti, *Wholly Falsetto with People Dancing*
Paul Vangelisti & Dennis Phillips, *Mapping Stone*
Allyssa Wolf, *Vaudeville*

All of our titles are available from Small Press Distribution.
Order them at www.spdbooks.org.